T0209171

Life
BEYOND
DEATH

Dr. Barbara Baron-Campbell

WESTBOW
PRESS®
A DIVISION OF THOMAS NELSON
& ZONDERVAN

WestBow Press books may be ordered through
booksellers or by contacting:

WestBow Press
A Division of Thomas Nelson & Zondervan
1663 Liberty Drive
Bloomington, IN 47403
www.westbowpress.com
844-714-3454

ISBN: 978-1-6642-6924-8 (sc)
ISBN: 978-1-6642-6923-1 (e)

Library of Congress Control Number: 2022911073

Print information available on the last page.

WestBow Press rev. date: 07/29/2022

To my parents, grandmother, nana, and my daughter, who passed from this life to the next. To my husband and family who supported me through the tough times in life. Also, to all my hospice patients, who taught me that death was just moving from one life to the next, and to those who have lost loved ones and struggle with whether they will see them again. Most of all to God, who is always with me.

CONTENTS

INTRODUCTION

This book is not a religious book or a scientific book. Rather, it explains the spiritual part of humanity when death approaches, which will encourage humanity. This book will illustrate that death is not the end but the beginning of something wonderful. I will discuss my experiences with short stories of hospice patients whom I served as chaplain. I will illustrate their experiences with life during the dying process. This will change your perspective on death and life.

PART 1
Stories

I entered Tim's—one of my patients—room one Monday and stood at the side of his bed. He said, "Don't stand in that spot. An angel's there."

As he said it, the angel disappeared. I asked Tim, "What did the angel tell you?"

"He said, 'Don't worry. Everything will be all right.' He told me I would going soon."

To my amazement, on Friday, when I came back to Tim's unit, I learned he had died that day.

Tim opened my eyes to the idea that angels were agents God sends to help people get ready to depart this physical world for a spiritual world and to help them not be afraid of the unknown.

Another patient I visited four weeks before he died told me that he had seen people in his room, one of which he assumed was a doctor because he was dressed in white including a white lab coat. I told him it was most likely an angel.

Two weeks after that, a patient had a dream that his wife, who had been dead for nearly ten years, was standing across a river near a mansion. He said that he had asked his wife if he could cross the river and that she had said, "No, not yet, but it'll be ready for you in two weeks."

Two weeks later, the patient passed.

This experience proves the existence of life beyond this physical world and that in the spiritual world is a house or mansion made specifically for the person dying, who will have to cross a river to get to it. Apparently, there are different areas in the heavenly realm.

One of my patients was a pastor who had knowledge of the afterlife. He was suffering from cancer and was in a coma; he was dying. When I visited him, his wife was there. When I was at his bedside, he opened his eyes and called for his wife to come closer. His face lit up with a smile, and he said, "I'm ready to go." His wife asked, "Where are you going?" He replied, "You know, with Jesus," and he breathed his last. God lets people know when He is coming for them.

One bedridden patient was dying at home; her daughter was there when I visited him. An antique clock in the living room had not worked in years; the patient had held onto it as it had belonged to her mother. Two days before she died, the clock began to work again and on the right time. At 5:30 a.m., the clock stopped, and at 6:30 a.m., the patient died. Outside her room on her windowsill were many birds that sang until the funeral home picked up her body.

In this case, the spiritual world connected with the physical by means of that clock. It started working again to allow her family to spend some time with her before she died. The birds were messengers to her family that she had left one world for another.

Birds are connected with God's plan for humanity; that's in Genesis with the flood story. Noah sent a bird out to seek dry land, and the bird returned to let Noah know when it was time to transition out of the ark to the world.

One patient who was dying of cancer and bedridden surprisingly got out of bed one day and told his mother to gather the family. All but one came, and the patient told his mother to tell him to hurry. When he arrived, the patient expressed his love for them and said that he was going to be in a wonderful place and that no one should worry about him. He returned to his bed.

The next day, his mother heard him having a conversation and went into his room. No one else was there, so she asked him whom he was talking to. He said, "You don't see them? Listen to what they're singing." She said that she saw no one and heard no singing. "Do at least see Jesus," the patient said. "He's standing right here, and the angels are singing 'Amazing Grace.'" He told his mother how much he loved her and uttered his last words: "Goodbye, Mom." He took his last breath then.

He seemed to have experienced two worlds before he died—the physical world and the spiritual world—the second heaven with the presence of Jesus. That prompted him to want to leave the physical world; he did not feel sad about leaving and disconnecting with his family though he loved them.

He had known when he would depart the physical world and was very fortunate in spite of the pain he was in to have full connection with the spiritual world.

One patient, a Muslim, really touched my heart. He was in a coma in a hospice unit, and his wife was at his side. A nurse had called me to say that he wanted to see a chaplain, which surprised me because his wife had previously told me that Muslims from his mosque would come to provide them with spiritual support.

When I visited them, his wife said that he had been unresponsive for three days. I got close to the bed and leaned over to speak to him since the last sense to leave was hearing. I said, "This is Barbara, the chaplain."

He opened his eyes, and his wife rushed over to the bed in shock. He looked at me and positioned himself to kiss my cheeks. He took my hand and said, "I have seen angels and the Lord Jesus." I had to compose myself because of his excitement. I knew he had seen Jesus. I was overwhelmed and didn't know what to say, but I offered some prayers.

The next day, I learned that he had died, and I called his wife to offer my condolences and find out how she was coping. She told me that after I had left his room, he had gone back into the coma and did not open his eyes again until he stopped breathing.

I had not developed a relationship with the patient because of his desire to rely on fellow Muslims for spiritual support, but he had connected with the spiritual world and Jesus while he was in a coma. As the scriptures say, "Every knee will bow, and every tongue confess that Jesus is Lord." He knew I was a representative of God and was thankful for my presence; that was why he had kissed me on the cheeks. He knew I was coming, and I wanted to know if he had seen Jesus. He had been able to switch from the physical to the spiritual worlds.

About four days later, his wife asked me if I would officiate his funeral, and I told her that I would consider that an honor. Her mother had requested that. What was so surprising was that his mother was a pastor in Michigan; she had been praying for years for her son to give his life to Jesus. I was so happy because I realized that the prayers of a mother for her children avail much. I also realized that God orchestrated my path to cross his so that the mother's prayers would be answered.

One afternoon when I was visiting a patient, she was in such despair. Crying, she put her hand on my shoulder. I began to caress her hair and asked, "What's wrong?"

She said, "My son is in jail, and look what's happening to me. I'm dying."

She turned and looked out the window and was gazing at something. I asked, "What are you staring at?"

"An angel is out there."

"Have you seen it before? Do you know what it wants?" I asked.

"I'm not sure what the angel wants," she said, "but I saw it when I was at Emory Hospital."

She kept crying and was hyperventilating. She again looked out the window and said, "Look! There's Jesus! He's telling me to calm down."

She did calm down, and her face was glowing.

A couple of weeks later, she transitioned out of the world.

She had been having a crisis thinking about her coming death and her son in prison. Apparently, the supernatural realm knew of her heartache because of her love for her son, whom she could not see. God knows how devastating such a situation can be. I did not see what she had seen out that window, but this proves that the spiritual realm knows everything happening in someone's life and understands the pain associated with it. The angel had tried to comfort her and prepare her for her transition, and then Christ Himself appeared because of His love for us and because there is peace and joy beyond what we see and feel.

One patient, Mr. B, affected my walk with God and my belief that heaven was a perfect place without suffering, pain, hate, prejudice, confusion, tears, heartache, disease, sickness, handicaps, shortcomings, no aging, and most of all, no death. Those who die with any sort of disability are healed. The flowers, grass, trees, and plants never die, and their beauty will take your breath away. Heaven operates like earth. I believe there are sports there due to the beautiful fields and grass so green and cut perfectly and bleachers full of people.

God wanted Mr. B to experience heaven before he transitioned, but he was unable to enter through the gate. God wants people to be at peace about leaving by knowing that their loved ones who had gone on before they did were waiting for them and knew what was going on with their loved ones on earth.

We can see from Mr. B's experience that his sister, who had died crippled, was in perfect condition and was waiting for him. She knew he was on his way as he was dying from a dreadful disease. What I did not know until Mr. B's death was that he had always been sad not knowing if his sister was still crippled. God's love and the relationship Mr. B had with Jesus gave Mr. B the confirmation he was looking for—his sister was not crippled in heaven.

God's love for humanity and for those who accept His Son as their Savior is unexplainable but boundless.

One Saturday morning, I woke up at 8:00 but went back to sleep, a deep sleep in which I saw my spirit leave my body and go through the clouds. I heard all types of voices while my spirit was ascending. I found myself standing in a beautiful manicured stadium with green grass. I saw many people sitting in the bleachers. It was so amazing. It is very hard to describe the overwhelming love I felt.

I saw someone wearing a beautiful long, white robe walking in the field. I realized it was the Lord. I ran to Him, dropped to my knees, and grabbed the bottom of His robe. I said, "Jesus, My Messiah."

He looked at me and told me some personal things and some trials I would face; He told me to keep my head up. The people in the bleachers were witnesses who heard our prayers and agreed with the prayer requests. They cheered me on telling me to keep doing the work for the kingdom.

The Lord told me I had to go back, but I said, "I don't want to go back!"

He said, "Your work is not done. I will be waiting for you—with a crown."

I found myself back in my bed by 8:30. I had spent thirty minutes with my Lord, but it had seemed like an eternity.

I kept this experience to myself until three weeks later, when I received a call from the RN, who told me that Mr. B wanted to see me as soon as possible. I visited him, and to my amazement, he told me that he had had a dream about heaven. He said that he was at the gate of heaven and saw his sister behind the gate with Jesus; he said that she was not crippled. He said that he had wanted to go through the gate but that Jesus had told him that it wasn't his time for that. He said that he had told Jesus that he just wanted to see what heaven looked like and that Jesus had told him, "Ask your chaplain."

That really surprised me, but I told him what I had seen of heaven in my dream.

Mr. B passed away about two weeks later.

PART 2

I want to relate my experience of losing a loved one and my friend's experience of losing a baby through miscarriages.

My dad, Edward Baron, got stomach cancer at age eighty. No one knew that at the time, but he was experiencing severe pain. My stepmom took him to the hospital, and he started doing better, so they were going to send him home.

While he was in the hospital, he dreamed that Jesus came to him and showed him a mansion. He said that when He was ready for him, He would come for him.

When Dad was released from the hospital, he was unable to hold any food down. He told me that he was ready to leave and be with God. He said that we had to continue with our lives because he would be all right.

Two days later, I was standing by his bedside when he raised his hands, stared up, and said, "Thank you, Jesus, for saving me and taking me with you." I asked him if he saw heaven, and he said yes. He lowered his hands and thanked God again.

The next day, he told me that he had seen his favorite uncle, who had died nearly forty years earlier. The uncle had told him to go and pray and then disappeared.

That night, my stepmom said, "I believe he's going soon."

I slept at my dad's bedside all night listening to the breathing as it began to decline. At 8:00 a.m., we all were getting ready to leave, take a shower, and come back, and I told Dad that. He called out my husband's name and said, "I love you."

As we were driving home that morning, I caught a whiff of my dad's odor and asked if anyone else smelled that. They all said no, but I definitely caught his aroma.

At 9:00 that morning, the nurse called with the sorrowful news that my dad had passed, so we turned around and went back to the hospice.

My stepmom called my brother, who had just woken up. He said he had just had a dream in which he had seen Dad dressed in white and smiling broadly. When we got back to the hospice, we learned that he had been pronounced dead at 8:49 a.m.

Animals can grieve for their loved ones too. The night before Dad died, his dog went into his garden and cried for about thirty minutes and would not come in; my stepmom had to carry him in. Three months later, the dog fell sick and was barely eating, and the week before his death, he didn't eat anything. My stepmom had a vision of Dad in a white suit with the dog, so when she woke up, she searched for the dog and found him dead.

This experience proves that when people pass, they just transfer from this world to the next and that they try to prepare others for their departure. It brings an awareness of an eternal afterlife with God, who loves us all.

Daughters have special connections with their mothers that make their mothers' passing particularly painful. Mothers and daughters have what I call an umbilical cord connection formed during their nine months in their mothers' wombs. A daughter's grieving her mother's death has its own language; she wants to hang onto her mother even after she has passed. It causes her to kneel and feel she is losing her mind; she wants to get in the coffin with her mother and be buried with her; she wants to connect to her mother's bones.

In 1 Corinthians 5:6–8 (KJV), we read, "To be absent from the body is be present with God." Daughters know that they will reunite in heaven with their mothers who have passed, but in the meantime, they experience grief to the point that they will plead with God to take their lives so they can be with their mothers again.

When my mother passed, I asked God to take me as well, and I dreamed that He told me, "My anointing will get you through this, and today, I want you to watch this particular minister."

When I woke up, I turned on the TV and listened to the minister encouraging other to be encouraged because God's anointing would bring them through.

A few weeks later, I dreamed about my mother coming to pick me up in a van. I told her, "Mom, I can't come with you now because I have a lot of work to do." She said okay to that, and I watched her drive the van into the clouds. That dream taught me that God knows all things about humanity, that He loves us all and is very concerned about our pain. When our loved ones leave this life, they are subject to God, who can give them assignments to be our guides and protectors back in the physical world.

A few months after my mother's death, I ached for her love and presence and cried uncontrollably. I cannot adequately describe the grief I felt. The pain I felt in my stomach reminded me of the umbilical cord connection I had had with her through which our blood had mixed. The grief can be so severe that it affects you physically to the point of even getting cancer.

Blood brings life, and it represents life. In Genesis 4:10 (NIV), we read, "The Lord said, what done? Listen you brother blood cries out to me from the ground." Blood connects us: Matthew 26:28 (NASV) reads, "For this is my blood, of the covenant, which is poured out for many for forgiveness of sins." That passage confirms the covenant between God and His people.

How many times have we disappointed our mothers? Many times I am sure, but the blood we shared formed a covenant between us and our mothers that causes them to love us unconditionally. It's the same with God through Jesus Christ. The umbilical cord that connects us with God is a spiritual cord, and we read in Ecclesiastes 4:12b (KJV) that a "cord … is not quickly broken."

The connections we have with our mothers have a spiritual side as well that not even death can break, though we can be separated by death and grieve for that reason until we are reunited in heaven. That should give us hope; our separation is temporary.

Even those who were given up for adoption or whose mothers died in childbirth feel that connection to their mothers, that covenant with their mothers. One of my patients, who had never seen her mother because she had died giving birth to her, dreamed of her mother. In it, her mother told her that everything would be all right, that angels would be coming for her soon and that they would be together in heaven. When she told me that, her countenance changed. I knew she was ready to die, which she did three weeks later.

I share a story here of someone who had experienced a miscarriage.

My Story by Dominique Dumervil

The indescribable void those who experience miscarriages feel is different for every woman, but all such women feel an incredible loss. I lost two sons.

When I think of my first miscarriage, I think of Jonathan, my little warrior. He would have been my first son.

The words I associate with my first loss are *failure*, *inadequacy*, *unworthiness*, *shame*, and *guilt*. I felt all that and more. My partner did nothing to make me feel better. When I came home from the hospital, he simply went to bed leaving me crying for hours in the living room.

The next day, I had to suck it up because I had other children to take care of. No sense in wallowing in self-pity. That was not our way. Besides, I wanted to compartmentalize my grief. Some of the asinine things people told me about my miscarriage to supposedly bring me comfort hurt me only more; I heard, "You're young" and "You'll have other children." One person had the audacity to tell me that a miscarriage was nothing, that it was not even a real baby. That was probably the cruelest of all the comments I heard, and it stuck with me. It took me a long time to find my new normal.

Later, when I lost my beloved David, who would have been my second son, I was overwhelmed by a feeling of fear. I was extremely stressed at my job and at home, and losing David sent me into a clinical depression though I didn't realize that then. I was tired all the time. I didn't partake in any activities except work and church. I had lost my joy. I was holding onto my faith by a thread because I was sad on the inside though I was functioning on the outside.

I was a Christian after all, and as a result, I allowed God only 90 percent access to me; I closed off the other 10 percent from Him and everyone else. That 10 percent was where I hid my hurt, shame, and my thoughts of my sons. I was the only one who had the key for that place ... Or so I thought.

God repeatedly asked me for that 10 percent, and I would adamantly refuse His request, but in time and due to His love and kindness, He started to piece together my shattered heart. After a long while, I started yielding more to the Holy Spirit. My faith was growing stronger, and I was starting to move forward.

One day while I was watching TV, I heard a preacher say, "Now is the time to forgive yourself. It wasn't your fault, and God will have a plan for you and your babies in heaven." I fell to the floor, and God continued to minister to me. I felt deliverance as I began to let go of the hurt, shame, bitterness, resentment, and pain I was carrying. God took the hurt I couldn't bear anymore.

That didn't happen overnight; it was a process, but I am glad that God did not give up on me. Only God could have entered that secret place in my life and begin healing me. He asked me to believe and trust that He could heal me.

Guess what happened two years later? My son Didier was born. He was truly a miracle baby. But the real miracle was the work that God had done in my heart. If that work had not been done, I don't think I would have had the courage to endure my last pregnancy and receive my precious gift—Didier.

My experience of losing loved ones was never easy, but I learned to continue living, and as time went on, my mind, heart, and soul realized that they were not coming back. It's difficult to separate God from humanity. He is the creator of all things because of His eternal love.

Ultimately, God decides when and how we leave this side of life just as He chose when we entered it. We can plead with Him for more time in this life, but the older we get and the more we experience supernatural contact with Jesus, the more we long to be with Him and enter an eternal life with no more pain, hurt, suffering, disappointment, sadness, sickness, hate, sin, aging, and death.

May you find comfort in this book knowing that God loves you and will continue to grace you during your times of loss as you wait to see your loved ones again.

ABOUT THE AUTHOR

Dr. Barbara Baron-Campbell has spent almost twenty years working with the dying as a spiritual care coordinator and bereavement coordinator in hospice. She is also a pastoral care counselor who has had supernatural experiences with the spiritual world. She earned her Bachelor of Arts from Beulah Heights University, Atlanta, Georgia; a Master of Divinity from

Interdenominational Theological Center, Atlanta; and a doctorate from Trinity International University of Ambassadors, Atlanta.

Printed in the United States
by Baker & Taylor Publisher Services